About Vocations and Ministries

Les Miller

NOVALIS

© 2012 Novalis Publishing Inc.

Cover design: Mardigrafe
Cover illustration: Anna Payne-Krzyzanowski
Interior images: pp. 9, 10: Plaisted; pp. 12, 26, 28, 31, 35, 40: W.P. Wittman; pp. 16, 41: Ingram; p. 22: Sisters of Providence of St. Vincent de Paul, Kingston; pp. 25, 43: Jupiter Images
Layout: Mardigrafe and Audrey Wells

Published by Novalis

Publishing Office
10 Lower Spadina Avenue, Suite 400
Toronto, Ontario, Canada
M5V 2Z2

Head Office
4475 Frontenac Street
Montréal, Québec, Canada
H2H 2S2

www.novalis.ca

Library and Archives Canada Cataloguing in Publication

Miller, Les, 1952-
    25 questions about vocations and ministries / Les Miller.

1. Vocation, Ecclesiastical--Juvenile literature. 2. Vocation (in religious orders, congregations, etc.)--Juvenile literature.   3. Vocation--Catholic Church --Juvenile literature. I. Title.   II. Title: Twenty-five questions about vocations and ministries.

BX2380.M55   2012 j253'.2   C2012-900811-7

Printed in Canada.

We acknowledge the financial support of the Government of Canada through the Canada Book Fund for business development activities.

5   4   3   2   1   16   15   14   13   12

TABLE OF CONTENTS

25 Questions... About Vocations and Ministries

A word from the author

Where do you think your life will take you? Will you get married or stay single? Do you want to work in an office or with your hands? Will you enter religious life or will you live as a lay person? These are all important life questions that we ask ourselves and each other as we grow up. God calls all of us to live lives marked by caring, joy, wisdom and faith. Living this way might take us to some unexpected places!

God calls us all to love in many different ways. In my life, responding to God's call has taken me into the classroom to be a teacher, into my parish to serve as a catechist and an extraordinary minister of communion, and into my home to be a husband and to be a father to my daughters.

This book offers a window to your future. You are preparing to answer God's call in your own life, so I hope these questions will prompt you to ask more questions. My prayer for you is that you will ask and keep on asking this question: What is God calling me to do? The answer will be your vocation and the ministry or ministries you will undertake.

Les Miller

1

What is a vocation?

Young people like you often ask themselves: What will I do when I am older? What type of work will I do? Should I marry? How will I be part of my community? The answers to these questions are found in many places. Pay attention when you hear about people who have interesting lives. Ask for advice from family, teachers and friends. Look at your own interests, gifts and talents. And pray to God to help you decide which path to follow. These steps are all part of finding your vocation.

A vocation is much more than a job or a career. Your vocation may include the work you do someday, but it's bigger than that: it's your life's path. Your guide on this path is Jesus. With the help of his teaching and wisdom, you will find your way in life. Your vocation may lead you to married life or to the single life. It might lead you to take on a special role within the Church – for example, as a religious sister or brother, a priest, or a missionary. And it might lead you to different types of work.

 "Vocation" comes from a Latin word, *vocare*, which means "to call." As Christians, we believe it is God who calls us to our life's path.

What does the Bible tell us about vocations?

One day, while Moses was tending his sheep on a mountain, God spoke to him from a burning bush. Moses' calling or vocation was to be a leader – to lead the Israelites out of slavery. Moses protested that he wasn't a good choice because he didn't speak well. But God knew better. Moses became one of the most important leaders in history! (Read the story of Moses' call in the book of Exodus in the Bible, especially chapters 3 to 14.)

Another person who found it hard to trust God's call was Jeremiah. God called him to remind the people of Jerusalem to obey their sacred law. Jeremiah said he was too young for this mission, because he was only a youth. The call to vocation can be challenging. God reminded Jeremiah that he would always be with him. (You can read about Jeremiah's conversation with God in chapter 1 of the book of Jeremiah in the Bible.)

Jesus called many different people to be his disciples, such as Peter, Andrew and Matthew. Most of them were ordinary people who made mistakes along the way. God works through us and strengthens us in our life's path no matter who we are or what we do. Before they got the call, Peter and his brother Andrew made their living as fishermen. Matthew was a tax collector. Their calls to serve God remind us that all of us are asked to live as Jesus wants us to live.

FROM FISHERMEN TO FOLLOWERS OF JESUS

 The vocation of Mary came at an event called the Annunciation (see chapter 1 of the gospel according to Luke). The angel Gabriel invited Mary to become Jesus' mother, and she said "Yes!" Mary's trusting response to God's call is a model for all of us.

Who has a vocation?

In the Catholic Church, we all have a vocation to love. That means we are all called to follow in the ways of Jesus. But that doesn't mean we all have to do the same things. Some people are called to be the best dad or mom they can be. Others

St^{te} Thérèse de Lisieux

serve God as single people. Whether you get married or stay single, Jesus is your companion on the journey. St. Thérèse of Lisieux reminds us that we don't need to do dramatic things in our lives. We can do small things with great love.

Some Catholics have a vocation to serve God's people in a special way, as priests, religious sisters or brothers, or **deacons**.

Lay people may have other key roles in the Church. We will explore many of these roles later in this book.

Can we have more than one vocation? Yes! For example, a married man who is an ordained deacon has a vocation as a husband and father as well as a vocation to the **diaconate**. For most people, their different vocations blend together into God's call to follow him faithfully.

 The word "vocation" is used in two ways in the Catholic Church. In one sense, we all have a vocation to live faithful, hopeful and loving lives as we follow Jesus. In the other sense, a vocation is a call to **religious life**, such as that of a religious sister or brother or a priest who is a member of a particular religious community.

How do I find out what my vocation is?

If your vocation is about God calling you, how do you hear God's voice? Very few of us are as fortunate as Moses, who heard God's call through a burning bush. It can be a challenge to figure out what God is calling you to do. St. Francis of Assisi spent time alone walking through the countryside, asking, "God, what would you have me do?"

Talk to your family, friends, **parish** priest and teachers. This is a question that might take years to answer. Keep asking yourself the question St. Francis asked.

God talks to us in many ways. One way is through our gifts. What gifts has God given you? If your gift is caring for people, that could be your vocation. If you love nature, maybe you are being called to work to protect God's creation. If you are good with children, your vocation may be teaching. It's not always easy to see your own gifts. Listen to what others say about you if you are not sure where you shine.

Here are some good questions to keep in mind as you explore your vocation:

- What are my special interests, gifts and talents?
- Is there a specific need for my interests, gifts and talents?
- Has someone told me I would be good at a certain type of work?

Listen for the answers. Over time, they will become clearer.

 Trying to find your vocation is called **discernment**.

Does God call young people like me?

Definitely! We have seen that young Jeremiah was called by God. In fact, all Christians are called at their Baptism to find the path to Christian life. In this sense, Baptism can be seen as a sacrament of vocation. With the help of your family and the Church community, you will be guided to find ways of living a good and holy life.

At Baptism we are given the privilege and duty to be like Christ, who is priest, prophet and king. That means you were joined to Christ in Baptism. Jesus is the ultimate priest, prophet and king. In your everyday life you can take on these roles in your own way.

The role of the priest in Jesus' day was to offer sacrifices to God. Jesus sacrificed his own life for us. We are called to offer our lives to God by being faithful to God's ways and loving those around us.

We are prophets when we tell others about Jesus' message. The best way to teach others about Jesus is through actions that are loving and just.

The best kings serve others, as Jesus served the poor and the outcast. You can claim your kingship in helping those in your family, classroom and community who are most in need.

By living as "priest, prophet and king," young people can begin to answer God's call to live good lives.

 Many young people have answered God's call to live saintly lives. They include Joan of Arc, Thérèse of Lisieux, Dominic Savio, Kateri Tekakwitha, and Pier Giorgio Frassati. Read about their lives on a Catholic website.

6

Is marriage a vocation?

Yes! Marriage is one way for Catholics to live their vocation to love. Choosing to marry is a big decision. The Church asks couples to take a marriage preparation course to help them understand that marriage is both a vocation and a sacrament. (For more about marriage as a sacrament, see *25 Questions about Sacraments*.)

Let's imagine that when you are in your 20 or 30s, you find you have a vocation to be married. You have discovered this by falling in love with someone. You want to share the rest of your life with this person and raise a family together. But wait! Being in love and knowing you have a vocation to marriage isn't enough to make the marriage a success. Like any other life course, actions and not just feelings are the key. A few skills and habits can help you to live out your married vocation better.

Three of these skills and habits are faithfulness, good communication and forgiveness. In marriage, you and your spouse promise to be faithful to one another. Faithfulness means that your love is always focused on your spouse and

your family. Other loves in your life, such as work and friend-ships, take second place. Good communication is essential, too. Married couples need to let each other know what they are thinking and feeling. By understanding each other, they can avoid conflict and be good models for their children. Even when we try to avoid it, though, conflicts happen in families sometimes. One of the most important virtues that Jesus taught was forgiveness. When couples want to heal a conflict, they tell each other how they are feeling and why. They also listen carefully to their spouse to understand the other side of things. Forgiveness comes when a person decides not to hold a grudge after being hurt.

 Karen Sunde, a playwright and actor, wrote, "To love is to receive a glimpse of heaven." What do you think she meant?

How is the single life a vocation?

Some people have a vocation to living the single life. They are called to love as single people in the world.

Being single allows someone to show Christ's love to a wide range of people. Through their work or in their spare time, they can devote themselves to helping others without having responsibilities to a spouse or family. Single people may take on key roles in their parish or community.

Many good men and women in the history of the Church have had a vocation to the single life. Some of the most heroic became saints. St. Giuseppe Moscati was an Italian doctor who neither married nor entered religious life. He served the poor and the sick with great skill and dedication. He later became a teacher who instructed other doctors. Those around him learned from his dedication to God. He is a great example of a person living out his vocation to the single life.

Jean Vanier is a Canadian example of being called to the single life. Instead of marrying or becoming a priest, he founded L'Arche, a worldwide organization of homes where people with developmental disabilities live with caring friends. For more about him, read *25 Questions about Catholic Saints and Heroes* or research him on the Internet.

How do people know if they are called to religious life?

Do you ever wonder if you have a call to religious life as a priest, religious sister or brother, nun or monk? Your teen and young adult years are a great time to begin to explore this call. For some people, the call to religious life may be heard only later in life. A vocation to religious life is a serious commitment, because you make solemn promises to God. Like marriage, this is a big decision! The process of making this decision is called discernment.

Imagine that an adult you trust, such as a relative, teacher or parish priest, says to you a few years from now, "I have noticed that you have a strong faith and like to serve others. Have you thought about becoming a priest [or, for girls, a religious sister]?" This question might catch you by surprise, or it might put into words something that has been in your heart for a while. You might reply, "I have thought about it a bit, but I'm not sure." The next step would be to spend some time with a religious community, getting to know them and their mission. You might go on a **retreat** with the community. You might spend time in prayer and in conversation with members of the community to learn more about their life and work. It's a good idea to do this a few times and to visit different religious communities to find one that is a good fit for you. After all, would you make a decision to marry someone after a single date?

Discernment involves prayer, reading and careful listening to the wisdom of spiritual leaders. During this time, you might work with a spiritual director. This person will help you discern whether you have a vocation to religious life.

If, after your time of discernment, you still think you have a vocation to religious life, you will go through a time of **formation** before you make your solemn **vows** to God before the community. During this formation period, you will learn more about what it means to be a religious in the world today.

 Spiritual directors work with anyone who wishes to deepen their relationship with God.

 Religious communities have excellent websites that describe their mission and tell you how you can learn more about them. Do some research on your own or with a friend or parent. Tell others what you have learned.

How does someone become a priest?

Any single Catholic man may be eligible to become a priest. A man first spends time in discernment (see Question 8) to find out if God is truly calling him to the priesthood. During this time, he lives a life of prayer and takes part in the sacraments and the life of the Church by being active in parish life. He may also spend time serving those in need in his community. In Canada, most men go to university first, then apply to a formation program. This formation takes place at a **seminary** in the **diocese** or in a religious community. It often takes five to eight years of study and formation before a man is ordained a priest.

Men can choose how they want to serve God through their priesthood. A diocesan priest serves the people of a region called a diocese. Some men join a religious order, such as the Jesuits or Franciscans. Religious orders usually have a particular mission or charism, such as teaching or serving the poor.

As part of their formation, seminarians spend time studying theology and other subjects and serve in a parish or religious community. Those who are in religious orders may also go to missions at home or abroad to serve God's people.

When the time of formation is over, a man is first ordained a deacon and then becomes a priest through the Sacrament of **Holy Orders**. In this solemn and meaningful celebration, the **bishop** ordains the new priest.

 In Canada, there are 52 dioceses and 18 **archdioceses**. An archdiocese usually serves a larger geographical area, has a larger number of Catholics, or is more historically significant than a diocese. What is the name of your diocese? Find out more about it by visiting its website.

??????????? **10** ???????????

How does someone become a religious sister or nun?

Catholic women can become sisters or nuns. There is a difference. A nun is usually a woman religious who lives in a **convent** or **monastery** and mostly lives away from society. A sister is a woman religious who is part of a religious community but spends much of her time serving others in the world. In the past, many sisters worked as teachers or nurses, but today they serve in lots of different professions.

To become a religious, a woman spends time in discernment: praying, serving others (perhaps working in a parish or with the poor), and seeking advice from wise people. She also spends time with the religious community she is interested in joining.

SISTERS OF PROVIDENCE OF ST. VINCENT DE PAUL WITH STUDENTS IN PERU

Once she decides to join the religious community, she goes through several stages before vowing to spend the rest of her life in the community.

- Step 1: She begins as a **postulant**, candidate or associate. During this time, she tries to figure out if religious life is for her. She may not be living in the convent or with other sisters at this time. The community is also looking to see if her gifts are suited to their community. This stage is a bit like dating: the woman and the community are getting to know each other and seeing if they have a future together.

- Step 2: If all goes well, she then becomes a **novice**. At this stage she is a member of the community and takes an active role in community life. She is committed to the religious order but hasn't taken her vows yet. This stage is like a couple being engaged before getting married: they have chosen each other, but they have not made a lifelong commitment in front of the community yet.

- Step 3: Finally, she takes her vows to become a lifelong member of the community. This stage is like marriage: a public commitment, for life!

Major Canadian religious orders for women include the Grey Sisters, the Loretto Sisters, the Sisters of St. Joseph, the Felician Sisters, the Carmelite Sisters, and the Congregation of Notre Dame.

Who are religious brothers and monks?

Religious brothers and monks are Catholic men who have decided not to marry but instead to dedicate their lives to God. Most do not become priests. Monks usually live in a monastery or abbey – a community that has limited contact with the outside world. Here monks pray and work together. Monasteries are models of Christian community, because they try to live as closely as possible the way that Jesus taught. Religious brothers live together in larger communities or in smaller houses. They usually serve the world around them rather than living apart from it.

Monks and brothers have played a key role in the history of the Church. In the early centuries of Christianity, they set up centres of learning. Some were teachers and scholars who wrote out copies of the books of their time by hand and kept these books safe for future generations. Others worked on farms or in kitchens, serving their community. In fact, the first universities were created by communities of religious men. A number of men started their own communities: St. Francis of Assisi founded the Franciscan orders, which faithfully serve the poor and the environment. St. Ignatius founded the Society of Jesus (the Jesuits), and St. Dominic

founded the Dominicans. Jesuit and Dominican brothers and priests were important teachers who spread the word of God throughout the world.

 The Franciscans have been given the special responsibility of looking after many of the sacred sites in the Holy Land, where Jesus lived.

Who is a deacon and what does he do?

Deacons are Catholic men who serve their diocese. There are two kinds of deacons: transitional deacons and permanent deacons. Transitional deacons are on the journey to priesthood. Permanent deacons will not become priests.

Many permanent deacons work in parishes, where they help the priest by celebrating Baptisms and presiding at weddings. They play an important role at Mass, too: they may proclaim the Gospel and give the homily, as well as assist the priest at the altar. Some deacons work in hospitals, in schools, in prisons or with homeless people.

In the early days of the Church, deacons

A DEACON GIVING THE HOMILY AT MASS

and deaconesses helped the apostles spread the gospel message and baptized new members of the Church.

Deacons may be married and have children. Men who feel they have a vocation to the diaconate contact their local bishop. If they are accepted, they take formation courses. This time of formation may take several years.

 Wives of deacons often join their husbands for this formation, because in many ways the vocation of the deacon affects the whole family.

What is a bishop?
What is an archbishop?

After the death and resurrection of Jesus, the apostles spread the gospel to many communities in the Roman Empire and beyond, leaving leaders behind to continue this work. These were the bishops. As Christian leaders, they were responsible for organizing Christians, teaching them about God's love for them, and making sure the community was faithful and holy.

As time passed, Christian communities covered a larger area. These areas were called dioceses. Dioceses were divided up into smaller areas, called parishes. Priests were responsible for the parishes. Some communities became so large that a single bishop could not properly oversee the work. They formed archdioceses, and were led by an **archbishop**. The Church is still organized this way today.

A BISHOP BLESSES THE PEOPLE

Bishops gather in provincial assemblies, national conferences and worldwide councils. Their role is to care for the people of their diocese and to guide the Church by their teaching. The most recent worldwide council of bishops was held in

Rome between 1962 and 1965. This was the Second Vatican Council. At the Council, bishops from around the globe made important changes in the ways we worship and how we interact with other Christians and other faiths.

 A bishop wears special robes. He also wears a pointed hat called a **mitre** and carries a staff called a **crosier**. The crosier is modelled after the staff a shepherd carries. This symbol connects the bishop to the role of Jesus, the Good Shepherd who cares for his flock. Bishops also wear a violet skullcap called a **zucchetto**.

(14)

What is a cardinal? What is a pope?

A cardinal is almost always a bishop or archbishop who is chosen by the pope. Usually there are between 100 and 150 cardinals around the world.

Most cardinals have leadership roles in the Church. They may oversee some of the valuable work the Church does in organizing the faithful, spreading the Gospel and serving the poor all over the world. Another key role for cardinals is to elect one cardinal to become the new pope when the pope dies.

The pope is the leader of the Roman Catholic Church. He serves people through his teaching, leadership and guidance. He is chosen by all the cardinals in an election and usually remains pope until he dies. For more on cardinals and popes, see *25 Questions about the Pope*.

 Catholic cardinals wear red robes. The songbird called the cardinal is named after the Church's cardinals because of the male bird's crimson feathers.

MINISTRIES IN THE PARISH

Many people respond to God's call by sharing their gifts in their parish. These forms of serving one another are called **ministries**.

What does an altar server do?

So far we have been exploring ways of living out your Christian vocation once you are an adult. But you don't have to wait that long – you can respond to the call of Jesus to serve and love God right now. Altar servers are boys and girls who help the priest as he presides at Mass.

Altar servers usually wear a white robe called an **alb**. They are part of the opening and closing processions: they may carry the crucifix, candles and incense burner used at Mass. They may hold the book of Mass prayers (called the Missal) so the priest can have his hands free to do the proper gestures. Altar servers also play an important role during the **Offertory**, preparing the altar for the Eucharist. In some parishes, they ring bells at key parts of the Eucharistic Prayer.

If you wish to become an altar server, talk to your parents or another trusted adult at your parish. Then talk to the parish priest with your family about serving on the altar. Some parishes have a training session for altar servers. Others ask you to accompany trained altar servers to gain experience.

 Although many altar servers are young people, there is no age limit. In some parishes, adults are the altar servers.

16

What is an extraordinary minister of communion?

A **minister** is a person who serves. In the Roman Catholic Church, the main minister at Mass is the priest. Normally, it is his role to distribute communion to all the people gathered for worship. Deacons also help to distribute communion. Other people may assist them. They are called "extraordinary" ministers of communion because the normal minister of communion is the priest or deacon.

These extraordinary ministers are trained in the proper way of giving communion. They also learn the deeper meaning of the Eucharist. Some of them have the special responsibility of taking communion to the sick, the elderly and others who cannot get to church for health reasons. During this visit, the minister prays with them, gives them Christ's body, and reminds them that they are an important part of the parish.

After extraordinary ministers of communion complete their training, the priest and the people at Mass pray a special prayer over them. This is called **commissioning** – it means they are given a mission or role in the community.

What is a minister of hospitality?

Ministers of hospitality have a number of jobs to do. First, they greet people as they arrive at church, making them feel welcome. If the church is crowded, these ministers may help people find a seat. They may also take up the collection during Mass. In some parishes, ministers of hospitality choose people to bring up the gifts (the bread and wine) in the offertory procession. When people leave the church after Mass, ministers of hospitality may hand out the parish bulletin. They also help with emergencies, such as when someone feels sick during Mass.

Being a person of hospitality is a key part of being a Christian. Making people feel welcome, showing them that they belong in God's house, is an important role. Sometimes our world is a harsh place. People experience conflict and pain. Ministers of hospitality offer a friendly and welcoming face to those who come to worship at church.

Men, women and young people may be ministers of hospitality if they are regular members of the worshipping community and show a mature faith. If you would like to be part of this ministry, talk to one of the ministers of hospitality at your parish.

18

How do music ministers serve the parish?

Are you musical? If you are, you can share this gift with your parish community by singing or playing an instrument at Mass. Music is an ancient and beautiful way to express our love for God. Miriam, the sister of Moses, played on the tambourine after the Israelites were freed from slavery to the Egyptians. King David played on a harp. Much of our modern music has its roots in music that was played or sung in church services. Music ministers carry on this long tradition as they help people praise and worship God.

They lead us in singing hymns, the psalm and acclamations. Music ministers help the assembly to pray and to praise God.

In many parishes, young people can join the church choir. Talk to a music minister about it after Mass if you'd like to join. In the meantime, you can practise singing in your school choir.

 Two famous ministers of music are Bach (1685–1750) and Mozart (1756–1791). They wrote church music that is still being played over 200 years later. Listen to some of their church music on YouTube.

What is a catechist?

A **catechist** (pronounced kata-kist) is a teacher who helps people of all ages grow in faith. You might find catechists at your parish leading children's liturgy and helping kids understand the Sunday readings. Other catechists may lead religious education classes at the parish or guide children as they prepare for the sacraments of First Communion, Confirmation or Reconciliation. Catechists also work with adults who will be baptized – called **catechumens** (kata-cue-mens) – or those who are already baptized and want to explore their faith more deeply.

Being a catechist is a challenging ministry. Catechists need to have an in-depth knowledge of the Catholic faith and a genuine love and care for those they teach. They also need to keep growing in their own faith. They show their love for the Church in their words and actions.

- As you grow older, you may feel a call to share your faith with others as a catechist. A good place to start is by assisting an experienced catechist. (This is also excellent training if you are thinking about becoming a teacher when you grow up.) As a catechist, you can grow in your faith by learning from other catechists and taking part in special training sessions.

What do the Knights of Columbus and the Catholic Women's League do?

Two other forms of parish ministry are the Knights of Columbus and the Catholic Women's League.

In 1882, an American priest named Fr. Michael McGivney started a men's group called the Knights of Columbus in his parish in Connecticut. The aim of this group was to help poor Catholic families, especially widows and orphans after the family breadwinner died. Over the years, this active group spread to many parishes in the United States, Canada and other parts of the world. The Knights support the local work of the Church. They meet regularly to pray together and do good works, such as raising money for the poor.

Many women join the Catholic Women's League in their parish. This group was founded in Montreal in 1917 by Bellelle Gueren, an accomplished poet. Before long there were so many women joining, it became a national organization. Bellelle became its first president. Members gather to support each other's faith life, to learn about and speak out on important faith issues, and to help the needy in the parish and the larger community. They actively promote social justice and respect for women as they work to end poverty, support women's projects in developing countries, and much more. Their mission is to call members to holiness through serving the people of God.

The Knights of Columbus and the Catholic Women's League give lay Catholic men and women opportunities to gather, pray and work together in parishes, in dioceses and at the national level. They help to build the parish community and continue the Christian mission of serving those in need.

Find out if your parish has a chapter of the Knights of Columbus or the Catholic Women's League. If the answer is yes, ask if you can speak to a member about their experiences. Or visit the groups' websites to learn more.

What is the parish council's role?

A parish may have one priest and a thousand parishioners. Lay people (those of us who are not priests or members of religious orders) make up most of the Church.

The pastor (the priest in charge) is the leader of the parish when it comes to spiritual matters. A parish council, which is mostly or all lay people, helps him to make sure the parish is running well by advising him and supporting him in his ministry. It also organizes and works with other groups in supporting the spiritual and social life of the parish. Parishioners elect some parish council members, while others may be appointed.

 Parish councils have been a key part of most parishes since the **Second Vatican Council,** in the 1960s.

VOCATIONS IN OUR EVERYDAY LIFE

How is being part of a family a vocation?

Our homes are the places where we first learn about love. Home is also where our love is tested the most! Our parents or guardians teach us how to be loving. Sometimes they use words, but most often they teach us by example. They show us that love involves patience and kindness. Over time, we grow into people who can return their love and kindness by being kind and generous to others. For example, we do chores around the house or yard or take care of younger brothers and sisters.

Through our parents or guardians, God calls us to be loving people. We respond by observing the fifth commandment: "Honour your parents." We practise love again and again in our families. Often we fail to love. We show our anger and frustration when we feel disappointed or misunderstood. In family life, we learn to overcome these problems. We learn to see things from the point of view of other family members. But there's more to love than just seeing the way others look at things. Love is put into action when we act on that new understanding. It is one thing to understand why your mom or dad finds that preparing and cleaning up after dinner is a big job after a long day at work. We put our love into action when we help with dinner or do the dishes afterwards without complaining.

One of the most important times for families to gather is at mealtimes. It is no accident that so many stories of Jesus involve meals. Can you think of one?

How is friendship a vocation?

Our vocation to love lasts our whole lives. Through our friendships, we develop our skills as loving people.

Usually it is easy to find friends. You share common interests or experiences. You have fun together. If you didn't, you wouldn't really be friends. But even best friends can have arguments or misunderstandings. These are times when you need help and wisdom. The scriptures and the wisdom figures in our Church can help you here.

Jesus told us many times that we need to forgive others (and ourselves!). We need to forgive our friends again and again. When a friendship gets bumpy, Jesus asks you to see beyond your hurt feelings. By forgiving your friends or asking them to forgive you, you accept that no one is perfect. That is why you need to be patient with yourself and with your friends.

Some things that happen are signs that a friendship may not be healthy. If someone you know asks you to do things you know are wrong, your **conscience** will tell you to reject their advice or pressure. When you obey your conscience, you are being a good friend. You show through your actions that there is a better way. We grow as people of conscience when we listen to the teachings of Jesus and the Church, as well as to the wise advice of adults we trust.

 Jesus says there is no greater love than to give up one's life for a friend (John 15:13). He teaches the value of looking out for the well-being of others before thinking about our own comfort.

How can students lead a Christian life?

As we saw earlier in this book, everyone is called to love God. We can always learn to love God more deeply by learning about God from our families, catechists, priests and teachers. Whether we are at school or at home, we can grow in our understanding of God by reading the Bible, finding out what the Church teaches, and exploring what it means to be a Christian. There is always more to learn about God.

The followers of Jesus were called disciples. They learned from the greatest teacher of all. He taught them using wise words and caring deeds. All Christians learn from Jesus, so we are all his disciples. At school, at home and at church, we can grow closer to God. In this sense, we never stop being students. Learning how to lead a Christian life is a lifelong journey.

Students who go to Catholic schools learn about their faith in religious education and other classes. They also learn about God's ways in school prayers and liturgies. The whole school tries to be a Christian community where every student is recognized as a member of God's family.

As of 2011, there were over 750 000 students in Catholic schools in Canada.

How is our sense of vocation supported?

No matter where your life takes you, you can find guidance by deepening your relationship with God. That means making sure you have a healthy prayer life. By taking time every day to be with God in prayer, you will show that you want to draw closer to God. Sometimes it is hard to pray. You might have other things you want to do, or you might not know what to say to God. This is where you need discipline. If you get in the habit of praying, you will stay on the right path. The greatest form of Catholic prayer is the Mass. Going to Mass every Sunday keeps us close to Jesus. Gathered with the community at Mass, we can ask for God's help as we try to respond to God's call to love in all we do.

If you think you might have a vocation to religious life, talk to your parents and then to a priest or religious sister or brother for support. When you are a little older, he or she can direct you to a person in your area called a **vocations director**. This person will help you find out how God is calling you. If you are called to religious life, the vocations director can help you take the next steps, such as going on retreats and spending time with people who are living religious life.

Alb: A white garment that is the sign of being baptized. Priests, deacons and altar servers wear albs at Mass.

Archbishop: A bishop who is responsible for a diocese that is geographically large, has a larger number of Catholics, or is historically important.

Archdiocese: The area that an archbishop oversees.

Bishop: The leader of a Catholic community in an area called a diocese.

Catechist: A person who teaches children or adults about the Christian faith.

Catechumens: People who are preparing to be baptized into the Church.

Commissioning: A special celebration or part of a liturgy when people are given specific roles in the Church.

Conscience: Our inner sense of knowing what is right and what is wrong.

Convent: A place where women who have made religious vows live.

Crosier: The tall staff that a bishop or archbishop carries at certain times.

Deacon: Ordained Catholic men (married or single) who serve their diocese.

Diaconate: A ministry of service in the Church. Members of the diaconate are called deacons.

Diocese: An area that a bishop oversees.

Discernment: The process of deciding how God is calling us to live out our vocation to love.

Formation: The time that those called to religious life spend as they prepare to take religious vows.

Holy Orders: A sacrament of the Church in which men become deacons, priests or bishops.

Lay people: All members of the church except those in Holy Orders and those in religious life.

Minister: A person who serves others.

Ministries: Ways a person can serve others in the parish through sharing their gifts, such as extraordinary minister of communion, music minister or altar server.

Mitre: The pointed hat that bishops (including cardinals and popes) wear.

Monastery: A place where religious men or women live. They are usually called monks or nuns.

Novice: The name given to those entering religious life as a sister, nun, brother or monk when they are in the early stage of their formation.

Offertory: The part of the Mass when the gifts (bread and wine) are brought to the altar.

Parish: A section of a diocese. The leader of a parish is a priest, called the pastor.

Pastor: The priest who is in charge in a parish.

Postulant: Someone in the earliest part of their formation who is trying to decide if they are called to live in a religious community.

Religious life: A vocation in which people make vows to serve God through their lives. A person who lives with vows is called a "religious."

Retreat: Time in a quiet place where you can pray and encounter God, usually in silence.

Second Vatican Council: An important gathering of the world's bishops and cardinals at the Vatican in Rome between 1962 and 1965.

Seminary: A place where men go for their formation to become priests.

Spiritual director: A person who helps others discern how God is calling them or acting in their lives.

Vocations director: An advisor who helps people discern how God is calling them, especially if they are thinking about entering religious life or the priesthood.

Vows: Solemn promises of poverty, chastity and obedience made by people who are entering religious life.

Zucchetto: A small, round skullcap worn by Catholic bishops, especially at Mass. Bishops and archbishops wear a violet one, cardinals wear a red one, and the pope wears a white one.

Printed on Silva Enviro 100% post-consumer EcoLogo certified paper,
processed chlorine free and manufactured using biogas energy.